SPENCER LOOMIS SCHOOL
1 Hubbard Lane
Hawthorn Woods, IL 60047

SPENCER LOOMIS SCHOOL
1 Hubbard Lane
Hawthorn Woods, IL 60047

COLONIAL PEOPLE

The Shoemaker

ANN HEINRICHS

Marshall Cavendish
Benchmark
New York

Other Marshall Cavendish Offices:

Marshall Cavendish International (Asia) Private Limited, 1 New Industrial Road, Singapore 536196 • Marshall Cavendish International (Thailand) Co Ltd. 253 Asoke, 12th Flr, Sukhumvit 21 Road, Klongtoey Nua, Wattana, Bangkok 10110, Thailand • Marshall Cavendish (Malaysia) Sdn Bhd, Times Subang, Lot 46, Subang Hi-Tech Industrial Park, Batu Tiga, 40000 Shah Alam, Selangor Darul Ehsan, Malaysia

Marshall Cavendish is a trademark of Times Publishing Limited

All websites were available and accurate when this book was sent to press.

Library of Congress Cataloging-in-Publication Data
Heinrichs, Ann.
The shoemaker / by Ann Heinrichs
p. cm. — (Colonial people)
Summary: "Explore the life of a colonial shoemaker and his importance to the community, as well as everyday life, responsibilities, and social practices during that time"—Provided by publisher.
Includes bibliographical references and index.
ISBN 978-0-7614-4798-6
1. Shoemakers—United States—History—17th century—Juvenile literature. 2. United States—History—Colonial period, ca. 1600–1775—Juvenile literature. I. Title.
HD8039.B72U663 2011
685'.310097309033—dc22
2009007938

Editor: Christine Florie
Publisher: Michelle Bisson
Art Director: Anahid Hamparian
Series Designer: Kay Petronio

Expert Reader: Professor Paul Douglas Newman, Ph.D., Department of History, University of Pittsburgh at Johnstown.

Photo research by Marybeth Kavanagh

Cover photo by Wolverhampton Art Gallery, West Midlands, UK/The Bridgeman Art Library

The Art Archive: Culver Pictures, 4; *The Granger Collection*: 8, 17, 41; *The Colonial Williamsburg Foundation*: 11, 18, 25, 35; *The Image Works*: World History/Topham, 15; Mary Evans Picture Library, 31; *North Wind Picture Archives*: North Wind/Nancy Carter, 27; *Alamy*: brt PHOTO, 33; *Getty Images*: Bridgeman Art Library, 39

Printed in Malaysia (T)

1 3 5 6 4 2

CONTENTS

ONE

Footwear for a New Homeland

Horses hooves clatter along the cobblestone streets. The cries of fish and fruit sellers echo down the lanes. A blacksmith's hammer clanks with the sound of metal on metal. Church bells chime the time of day. In the background, soft and steady, is the tap-tap-tap of the shoemaker's hammer. These are the sounds that filled the air in a **colonial** town.

America's colonial times began around 1600 and lasted until 1783. That was the year the **colonists** won their independence. Before that they were under the rule of England. Thousands of colonists had sailed across the Atlantic Ocean from England to the American **colonies**. Many hoped to become wealthy. Some were seeking religious freedom. Most just wanted to start a better life

Colonial American towns and cities were busy places. People relied on the skills and products of their craftspeople.

for their families in a new land. They settled into thirteen colonies along the Atlantic coast. Among them were shoemakers with their trusty tool kits.

Crafts in the Colonies

The shoemaker was an important craftsman. Some colonists rode on horseback or took horse-drawn carriages for long trips. However, it was more common for people to walk miles on foot. They needed sturdy, well-made shoes because the roads and paths were often hard to walk on. Farmers needed shoes to protect their feet in the stubbly fields. For **merchants** in town, finer shoes were a sign of success. Shoes were certainly required for church services and town meetings. The shoemaker supplied proper footwear for all these needs.

Shoemaking was just one the many crafts that helped the colonies prosper. It took a great number of special skills to build a new homeland. Colonial leaders wrote back to England asking for all sorts of craftspeople. They needed carpenters, shipbuilders, and blacksmiths. They needed coopers to make barrels and wheelwrights to make carriage wheels. Tailors, shoemakers, bakers, printers, and metalworkers were all in demand. In fact, the top three occupations in the Virginia colony were shoemaker, tailor, and carpenter.

The Cordwainers' Guild

In England shoemakers had been respected craftspeople for centuries. There they were known as **cordwainers**. That name comes from cordwain or cordovan, a fine goatskin leather from Córdoba, Spain.

Shoemakers in London, England, formed the Worshipful Company of Cordwainers in 1272. This was a guild, or craft association. It governed the profession and made sure its members did quality work. The guild also oversaw the training of **apprentices**. A boy began his shoemaking career as an apprentice, learning his craft from a master shoemaker. After several years of training, he became a **journeyman** shoemaker. Then he could work for wages and seek work from other masters. Eventually, a journeyman might save enough money to open a shop of his own. Shoemakers in the American colonies continued this system of training. Many women and girls took part in shoemaking tasks, such as sewing. However, as in England, shoemaking remained a job mainly for men and boys.

Women in the Trades

Although female tradespeople were not as numerous as males, women and girls did take part in many colonial trades. There were female bakers, tailors, and shoemakers and even female blacksmiths and metalworkers. That is because businesses were often run by family members. Tradesmen taught their skills to their wives, sons, and daughters. When there was an increase in customers, everyone in the family would pitch in to help. Boys were taken on as apprentices, but sometimes girls were, too. A woman often took over her husband's business after he died. Replacing the master, she became the mistress of the shop.

One member of the Worshipful Company of Cordwainers was Captain John Smith. The guild helped pay for Smith's voyage to the Virginia colony. Landing in 1607, Smith became a leader in the Jamestown settlement. It would be the first permanent English settlement in the future United States and home to America's first shoemakers in 1610.

Cobblers and Shoemakers

Early settlers brought their own shoes from England. In their new land they met American Indians who wore moccasins— soft, heelless shoes made from animal hides. Some settlers began wearing moccasins, too, when they could not find English shoes. Some made shoes and clothing with buckskin from the deer they hunted. Others raised cattle and made crude shoes from hides and skins. Still, many colonists continued to wear shoes they imported from England. In the remote countryside they welcomed the arrival of the **itinerant** cobbler, a craftsman who repaired shoes.

In some colonies itinerant cobblers traveled from one settlement to another. In return for food and lodging, they patched and mended shoes. They also brought news about other settlers and about what was going on in town. Some cobblers also made shoes from the customers' own cowhides. Thus, the difference between cobblers and skilled shoemakers was sometimes blurred in remote areas.

In larger cities and towns shoemakers opened shops. Some shops were next to or even attached to their homes. The shoemaker's shop faced the street or the village square, where other merchants and shopkeepers were located. In the back of the shop was the shoemaker's home. Some craftsmen also had crop fields and kept farm animals such as milk cows, pigs, goats, and chickens. Shoemakers' shops could be tiny. In the far-northeastern New England colonies they were called ten footers because they measured 10 feet on all sides. However, most shoe shops were larger because they had to be big enough for several workers and family members to live in.

The earliest known colonial shoemakers arrived in Virginia in 1610. The first one whose name was recorded was Christopher Nelme, who landed in Jamestown in 1619. He brought with him two hundred pairs of shoes, as well as shoemaking tools and supplies. That included two thousand thin, headless nails called sparrow bills. In Massachusetts the earliest known shoemaker was Thomas Beard. He arrived in Salem, Massachusetts, in 1629. Beard brought with him a supply of hides and a kit of shoemaker's tools. After he set up his shoe shop, he got new hides from settlers who raised cattle. By the 1630s several shoemakers had opened shops in Boston, Massachusetts. Meanwhile, Virginia's shoe industry was thriving. By the 1660s the colony had at least sixteen shoemaking establishments.

Colonists had to be thrifty and spend money carefully. They tried not to wear out their shoes. In farming areas children went barefoot all summer. Stories have been handed down about people walking barefoot into town to attend Sunday church services. Only when they reached the churchyard did they put their shoes on. Shoemakers were proud to make such precious goods. They served their neighbors well and held a place of honor in the community.

The shoemaker's shop was built so it faced the street. This re-created shop is located in historic Colonial Williamsburg in Virginia.

TWO

The Shoemaker Begins His Day

Roosters are crowing at the first light of dawn as the shoemaker rises from his straw-filled mattress. Already he can smell the aroma of hasty pudding. His wife is cooking it in a big iron kettle over the fireplace.

As the shoemaker's family gathers around the wooden table to eat, another boy joins them. He is the shoemaker's apprentice. This boy's parents have agreed that he will serve the shoemaker for five to seven years. During that time he will learn almost every detail of the shoemaker's art. In return the shoemaker will give him a home, food, and clothing and also will teach him reading, writing, and arithmetic. The apprentice eats and sleeps in the shoemaker's home, just like a member of the family. However, he spends his days working in the shoemaker's shop.

Making Hasty Pudding

Hasty pudding was sometimes called corn mush. It was a porridge that colonists ate for breakfast, lunch, or dinner. They brought their recipes from England. Hasty means "quick," but it took a long time to make hasty pudding. Some cooks kept it boiling for hours. Here is a hasty pudding recipe that does not take long. Be sure to have an adult nearby to help.

Things You Will Need

3 cups water

½ teaspoon salt

½ cup cornmeal

Honey, syrup, or molasses

Directions

1. Put 2 cups of water in a pan on the stove. Heat it until it boils.

2. Put 1 cup of cold water in a bowl, and mix the cornmeal into it.

3. Add the salt to the boiling water.

4. Stir the cornmeal mixture into the boiling water.

5. Turn down the heat, and cook for 10 to 15 minutes. Stir often to keep it from sticking.

6. Remove the pudding from the stove, and spoon it into a bowl.

7. Stir in honey, syrup, or molasses to make it sweet.

Morning in the Shoemaker's Shop

After breakfast the shoemaker and his apprentice walk the short distance from home to the shop. In rural areas shoemakers often worked inside their homes or in a nearby shed. In larger cities and towns the shoemaker's shop faced the street and was alongside other merchants' shops. The work crew consisted of one or more apprentices, as well as journeymen and family members.

The shoemaker folds back the wooden shutters on the windows and unbolts the door. Looking out, he sees his sign, a big wooden shoe swinging from brackets above the door. In larger cities merchants advertised their services with pictorial signs. For example, a tavern's sign might show a bowl and a jug. This announced that people could find food and drink inside. The hatter's sign might be a wooden hat, and the tailor's sign, a large pair of scissors. A big, wooden cart wheel was the sign of the wheelwright's craft.

Putting on his leather apron, the shoemaker checks his supplies of leather and thread. Upper leather, for making the upper part of a shoe, is soft and flexible. It usually cost more than the thick, tough leather for the soles, or shoe bottoms. Then he brushes off his bench before the day's work begins. Every shoemaker's shop had a long bench. On one end was the seat where the shoemaker sat as he worked. Placed within easy reach to his right were the tools and supplies he needed.

The Customer

Soon the first customer of the day arrives. The shoemaker shows him an array of ready-to-wear shoes for sale that are hanging from the ceiling and in the windows. The shoemaker has made these shoes with the help of his journeyman shoemaker.

The colonial shoemaker worked while seated on a long bench. On his right, shoemaking tools were within easy reach.

An Apprentice's Contract

Orphan children were sent out to work as apprentices and learn a trade. So were children from poor families that could not afford to raise another child. The conditions of service for both boys and girls were often drawn up in a legal contract called an indenture. This document outlined the rights and duties of both parties. The term of service usually lasted until the apprentice's age of majority, or adulthood. For girls that was eighteen years old, and for boys it was twenty-one years old.

After looking at the shoes on display, the customer chooses a style. However, none of the shoes are in his size. He wants a new pair made from scratch. Making shoes according to a customer's order is known as doing bespoke work. Once the craftsman and the customer agree on a price, the shoemaker measures the customer's foot with a size stick and a tape measure. A good pair of shoes, well cared for, might last for two years, so a proper fit was important. In the 1600s several people in the Connecticut colony complained that a shoemaker was making shoes that did not fit. A court then ordered that all shoemakers in the colony use size sticks that had the same standard markings.

The Shoemaking Process Begins

Now the shoemaker starts to work. For the uppers he needs to select three pieces of leather—the vamp and two quarters. The vamp is the front part of the shoe, covering the toes and the top of the foot. The quarters are the sides of the shoe, which wrap around and join in the back. He also needs leather for the insole—the inner sole that is next to the bottom of the foot. Using a tool called a clicking knife, the shoemaker cuts out the shoe pieces.

Sewing the three upper pieces together is fine work. It requires a sharp eye, a steady hand, and the ability to make small, exact

Customers had the choice of purchasing ready-made or custom-made shoes. The gentleman in this illustration tries on a pair for size.

stitches. In rural areas, where the shoemaker worked at home, he might have his wife or daughters do this work. A city shoemaker often had women or girls do the stitching, too. Some shoemakers sent out the upper pieces to professional shoe closers, who did the stitching at home.

Next, the shoemaker chooses the proper size of **last**. The last is a wooden, foot-shaped form used for shaping shoes. Racks in the shoemaker's shop hold rows and rows of lasts in different styles and sizes. Taking a seat at his bench, the shoemaker attaches the last to his left thigh with a leather strap. This leaves his hands free to work with the leather.

A leather strap holds a last in place in this re-created colonial shoe shop. The strap enables the shoemaker to work with both hands.

After laying the insole over the bottom of the last, the shoemaker hammers a few tacks halfway in to hold it in place. Then he centers the upper leather on top of the last. Using special shoemaker's pliers, he pulls and stretches the upper tightly over the edge of the insole. This is an important step. The upper has to be kept perfectly smooth, with no creases or wrinkles. He hammers more tacks into the upper. This holds the upper in place until it is sewn.

Next, he sews on the welt. This is a strip of leather about 1 inch wide. It runs around the rim of the shoe's bottom, with the edge of the welt sticking out a little beyond the upper. Finally, he sews the upper, insole, and welt together, sewing through all three layers of leather, and removes the tacks.

A Community Gathering Place

Shoemaking was often called the gentle craft. It was calm, quiet work, unlike the noisy labors of carpenters and blacksmiths. The shoemaker mostly worked while sitting down, and his tasks left him free to think and talk. Thus, the shoemaker's shop was a common gathering place for people in the community. Throughout the day visitors dropped by to share local gossip and the news of the day.

Religion and politics were common topics. On Monday mornings the preacher was a likely visitor. He might stop by to discuss his

The Revolutionary Shoemaker

George Robert Twelves Hewes (1742–1840) was born into a poor family in Boston, Massachusetts. His father died when he was a child, and at age fourteen, his mother apprenticed him to a shoemaker. When he turned twenty-one, he opened his own shoemaking shop.

British soldiers occupied Boston in 1768, and Hewes soon became swept up in the colonies' fight for independence. Two years later he witnessed British troops firing on a group of citizens in an incident called the Boston Massacre. In 1773 Hewes joined other Bostonians in dumping a shipload of British tea into Boston Harbor. This became known as the Boston Tea Party. Once the Revolutionary War began, Hewes served as a soldier and a sailor.

As a shoemaker with many children to support, Hewes was always struggling on the brink of poverty. After the Revolution he moved his family to New York State and took up farming. By the 1830s Hewes was one of the last survivors of the Revolutionary War. The writer James Hawkes discovered him and wrote his biography, *A Retrospect of the Boston Tea-Party*. The book made Hewes a celebrity in the last years of his life.

Sunday sermon with the shoemaker and ask his opinion. Other visitors might discuss the political situation in the colonies.

By the mid-1700s many colonists were getting restless. They imported many of the goods they needed from England. But England was charging taxes on those goods to help pay for its wars with other European powers. The colonists resented these taxes because they had no representatives who could vote in England's parliament, or lawmaking body. Many colonists began to demand "no taxation without representation!" Some newspapers were urging colonists to buy clothing and tools from local tradesmen instead of buying English goods.

In the shoemaker's shop, visitors exchanged opinions about what to do. Some believed the colonies benefited from English rule. Others were angry. They thought the colonies should break with England and declare independence. In time this feeling would lead to the Revolutionary War (1775–1783).

THREE

A Good Day's Work

By midday it's time for dinner. The shoemaker's wife sends over a tray laden with freshly baked bread, creamy butter, bowls of stew, and a jug of apple cider. The shoemaker discusses the morning's work with his apprentice and journeyman and outlines their duties for the rest of the day. More visitors stop by to discuss politics, business, or the weather.

As he chats, the shoemaker works, often stopping to give directions to his workers. Shoes are taking shape as the day unfolds. The shoemaker has been coaching his apprentice in making the second shoe. Journeymen often assisted with these instructions, too. The master does some tasks himself, such as stretching the uppers around the last. Other tasks, such as sewing and polishing, he trusts to his apprentice and journeyman.

Finishing the Shoes

For the soles the shoemaker cuts out thick leather with a straight-bladed knife. Then, seated at his bench, he lays a lapstone on his lap and places a dampened sole on the stone. The lapstone is an oval rock that is smooth, flat, and about 10 inches wide. Lapstones often came from a seashore, riverbed, or stream, where the water had worn them smooth. Using a dome-faced hammer, the shoemaker beats the sole leather until it stiffens. Finally, it is ready to attach to the shoe.

He tacks the sole to the insole in a few spots, matching the edges of the sole with the edges of the welt. Now it is time to sew. The shoemaker's thread is called **waxed ends**. It is usually made of flax, the same plant fiber used to make linen cloth. Sometimes in colonial America, however, the finishing thread was made of rope. Several strands of the fiber are twisted together and coated with shoemaker's wax, which was made of pine pitch, rosin, and fat. Shoemakers did not use needles for sewing. Instead, they took a long length of thread and attached to each end a bristle from the coat of a wild boar, twisting the pieces together tightly with shoemaker's wax. The stiff, pointy bristles were thinner than needles, and they made sewing easier.

To stitch on the sole, the shoemaker first uses a pointed tool called an **awl** to pierce a hole through the sole and the welt. Then he sticks both bristles in the hole at once, inserting them from opposite sides. He pulls the thread through, then pierces the next hole and sticks both bristles through. This makes a strong, tight, double-sided stitch called a shoemaker's stitch.

Now the pair of shoes is almost done. As the day's light grows dim, the shoemaker lights candles around the shop. They are made from tallow, or beef fat heated to remove impurities. Tallow candles were smoky and had an unpleasant smell. Still, they were a much-needed light source for people who worked at night.

The shoemaker cuts out several layers of leather to make the heels. He stitches the layers together, hammers in shoe pegs to hold the top layer of the heel in place, and has the apprentice complete the work. The apprentice files down any pegs that stick through the insole. He also shaves any rough or ragged edges off the sole. Then he uses a piece of broken glass or even so-called sharkskin to smooth the edges of the soles and heels. "Sharkskin" is really the rough skin of a stingray. It works like sandpaper, making the sole and heel edges smooth. Finally, the apprentice uncorks a bottle of blacking. He polishes the shoes with this inky liquid until they shine.

Hammering the heels in place was one of the final steps in the colonial shoemaking process.

What Did it Cost in Colonial Times?

It is difficult to convert prices from colonial times into today's dollars. However, it can be useful to compare the prices of various goods and services at the time. Although the value of money varied by time and place, we can get a rough idea of how much of a person's income was spent on needed items. These figures are based on colonial records.

Item or Service	Date	Location	Quantity	Price
Minister's salary	1754	Connecticut	1 year	£140
Schoolmaster's salary	1759	Virginia	1 year	£60
Schoolmaster's salary	1737	New York	1 year	£40
Oxen	1728	New Jersey	1 pair	£6
Horse	1728	New Jersey	1	£5
Saddle	1755	Virginia	1	£2
Young lady's dancing lessons	1719	Boston	4 months	£2
Men's shoes	1721	Philadelphia	1 pair	6s. 6d.
Women's shoes	1721	Philadelphia	1 pair	5s.
Carpenter's wages	1712	Boston	1 day	5s.
Butter	1755	Virginia	1 pound	4d.

NOTE: 1 pound (£) = 20 shillings (s.), and 1 shilling = 12 pence (d.).

Paying for the Shoes

Throughout the day customers come in to buy ready-made shoes or to pick up shoes they have ordered. Some pay with pounds, shillings, and pence of English money. How much did shoes cost? That varied from place to place and from year to year, and there was a huge variety of prices and qualities to choose from. In 1721 the Pennsylvania colony fixed a limit of "six shillings and six pence for a pair of good, well-made men's shoes." In Virginia the average pair of shoes cost 5 to 6 shillings in the mid-1700s. That was equal to about one day's wages. Spanish silver dollars were commonly used in the colonies, too. Only in 1792 did the new United States establish the U.S. dollar as its official currency.

In colonial America a pair of men's shoes might cost five or six shillings.

Money was scarce in the colonies, though. Especially in rural areas, many customers paid the shoemaker by means of **barter**. That is, they gave him goods or services in exchange for their shoes. Shoemakers might take their pay in the form of crops, firewood, butter, cheese, honey, beeswax, or apple cider. A farmer might pay for a pair of shoes with a bushel of wheat, two bushels of corn, or five quarts of milk. In the Virginia colony the major product was tobacco.

Virginia passed a law in the 1660s setting the price of a pair of shoes at 30 to 35 pounds of tobacco, depending on the shoe size. In that case the customer registered this amount of tobacco as a credit for the shoemaker in a tobacco warehouse. The shoemaker might then use his tobacco credit to purchase something else in the future.

Some rural customers paid with labor. In exchange for a pair of shoes, a farmer might promise that he or his sons would harvest the shoemaker's crops. A man might promise that his wife or daughters would spin wool for the shoemaker's family or make flaxen thread for sewing shoes. One colonial customer offered a day's housework from his daughter in exchange for shoes.

By 7:00 or 8:00 PM, the shoemaker's workday is almost done. He has his apprentice put some sole leather into a tub of water to soak. This will soften it up for the next day. Then he puts his tools away and checks his account books as the apprentice sweeps the floor. At last, they shutter the windows, snuff out the candles, bolt the door, and go home.

FOUR

The Shoemaker's Community

Many newcomers to the colonies settled in the wilderness. They chopped down trees to clear the land and built sturdy log homes. For food they planted crops, gathered wild plants, hunted, and fished. Their cattle, sheep, goats, pigs, and chickens provided milk, meat, wool, hides, and eggs. Each family made much of their own clothing, furniture, and tools by hand.

Life was much different in colonial cities and towns. Families there did not have to take care of all their own needs. Instead, various merchants and artisans provided the whole community with special goods or services. Tailors and dressmakers sewed clothing for their customers. Bakers prepared buns and breads, and **apothecaries** mixed up medicines. Butchers sold fresh meat, and blacksmiths made horseshoes and other iron goods.

Dividing up the work this way made life easier. People depended on the skills of others, so no one had to do everything. Shoemakers were no exception. They provided shoes for the whole community. In turn, they depended on many others who practiced their trades along the cobblestone lanes.

The Leather Tanner and the Currier

The leather **tanner** was one of the shoemaker's most valuable suppliers. He turned raw animal hides into soft, smooth leather. The word *tan* comes from tannin, or tannic acid. This is a material found in the bark of certain trees. Hemlock, oak, willow, chestnut, and sumac were some of the best barks to use. The tannin toughened the raw hides so they would not rot or tear easily.

First, the tanner had to grind up the bark. He took a large, round, flat stone with a hole in the center and put a wooden pole through the hole. He attached one end of the pole to a post and the other end to a ring on a harness worn by a horse. Then he scattered the bark on a wooden platform on the ground. As the horse walked around in a circle, the heavy stone turned, passing over and over the pieces of bark. This mechanical action ground the bark into a coarse powder.

Meanwhile, the hides were prepared for tanning. The country tanner bought his hides from farmers, hunters, or butchers. The city

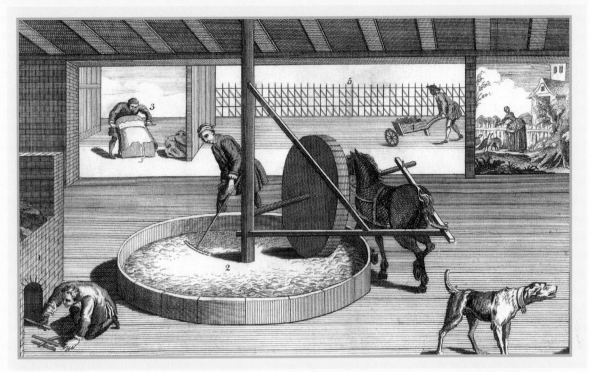

The tanner used a grinding stone to grind up bark for tanning the leather.

tanner got hides and skins from skinners or other local suppliers. The hides might come from deer, cattle, horses, or goats. Cowhide and calf skin were the most common hides used for shoemaking. The hides were soaked to loosen the hair. Then they were scraped to remove all hair, wool, and flesh.

The next stage took place at the tanning pits. These were large holes in the ground that were filled with water. Many tanneries were located near streams for a steady water supply. The tanner put the powdered bark into the water to draw the tannin out. Then he put the hides in to soak. Hides of different kinds took varying amounts of time to tan. The finer hides for shoe uppers might take about three months. Tough hides for the soles might have to soak for a year or more.

Next, the **currier** began his job. Using a knife, he scraped the underside of the hide to make it smooth and even in thickness. Then he rubbed in sheep tallow, codfish oil, and other ingredients to make it softer and more durable than plain tanned leather. The finished product was first-rate leather, fit for the finest shoe.

Leather Laws

Several colonies had laws governing the leatherworking trades, all based on the London Leather Act of 1603. In 1642 a Massachusetts court declared: "That no butcher, currier or shoemaker should be a tanner; nor should any tanner be a butcher, currier or shoemaker. . . . That no gash in a hide should be permitted. . . . That every hide should be well tanned." Violators had to pay stiff fines.

The New Hampshire colony passed a similar law. It also barred shoemakers from using poor-quality leather. The leather sealer, a town official, inspected all leather before it left the tanner or currier. Sealers in New Hampshire were paid one penny for each hide they inspected. Laws like those of Massachusetts and New Hampshire were meant to protect each trade and to ensure quality products.

The Last Maker

The last maker was a special kind of woodworker. He carved wooden lasts, the models used for shaping shoes. This was a highly skilled craft of sculpturing because a foot is so complicated.

Last makers used beech wood for lasts. Other woods were too soft or not tough enough. Using hand tools the last maker carved, chipped, and smoothed blocks into foot-shaped sizes. As a final step he bored holes in the ankle end of the last. By inserting

Lasts, or wooden forms the shoemaker used for shaping shoes, were carved by the last maker.

hooks in the holes, the shoemaker could pull the last out of the finished shoe.

Shoemakers needed several sizes of lasts for different foot sizes, and each size had a number. The smallest lasts, for children's shoes, were about 4 inches long. Then each size was longer by about one-third of an inch. For sizes falling in between the standard numbered sizes, the shoemaker would glue layers of leather to the last's toe or heel to make it longer. Later, last makers produced many more sizes.

The Merchant's Store

The merchant's store was one of the busiest shops in a colonial town. People went there to buy a variety of goods for their homes and businesses. There were sugar and flour, coffee and tea, pots and pans, and soap. There were hoes, axes, saws, hammers, and nails. The merchant imported goods in bulk, or large quantities, from England. Around his store stood big barrels of molasses, vinegar, and nails. Stacked in a corner were 100-pound sacks of salt. Flour and coffee beans came in big bags, too. Jugs, bottles, and boxes lined the shelves. Tables displayed bolts of gingham, muslin, calico, and other fabric used for making dresses.

The shoemaker got his hammers, awls, and other tools from

The merchant's store was full of supplies for all members of a colonial community.

the merchant's store. Some shoemakers bought their waxed ends, or shoemaker's thread, there as well. Others made it themselves. They might buy thread, wax, and wild boar bristles at the store. Then they waxed the thread and attached bristles to the ends.

Like other colonial tradespeople, the merchant often took crops or other goods in trade. He could, in turn, sell those goods. The store provided a simple kind of banking service, too. A customer could buy things on credit, promising to pay later. The storekeeper kept track of those deals in an account book. This was a written record of what each customer bought, owed, and paid. Many of those stores also served as post offices where people could pick up their mail.

This was an early stage of community development in the colonies. Banks, post offices, grocery stores, and hardware stores later took over the merchant's many roles. Shoemaking, too, would soon grow beyond the small-scale shoemaker's shop.

FIVE

A Changing Craft

Shoemaking began to change after the Revolutionary War. The former colonies were now a union of independent states. They could no longer rely as heavily on English goods or skilled workmen coming from England. This change forced many American industries to become more efficient. The population in the new United States was growing fast. Shoemakers and other craft workers had to produce more goods, and to make them faster and cheaper than ever.

Some customers still demanded custom-made shoes. They liked having the neighborhood shoemaker measure their feet and make shoes that fit just right. They knew a master craftsman was involved in every step of the process. However, the growing country needed large-scale production of ready-made shoes. The days of the small-scale shop were coming to an end. Shoemaking was becoming a mass-production industry.

Mass Production: Splitting Up the Tasks

Many shoemakers began doing **wholesale** work. That is, they made great quantities of shoes to sell to stores. Lynn, Massachusetts, which had become a center for making women's shoes, led the way in wholesale shoemaking. Virginia, New York, Pennsylvania, and other states had growing shoe industries, too.

Shoemakers opened larger shops and hired many more journeyman shoemakers. The tasks were split up, with each worker performing one job over and over. One might cut out all the leather. Another might sew on all the soles. Journeymen were often given work to take home. They might attach a half dozen soles at night and bring them back the next day.

With the demand for workers, women and girls got even more involved in shoemaking. They were good at sewing the three parts of the shoes' uppers together. For this they were paid 3 to 5 cents a pair. Some women worked in the shops, while others worked at home. Children—both girls and boys—became an important part of the shoemaking labor force.

Naturally, the apprenticeship system declined. There was no point in spending years training someone in every aspect of shoemaking. A journeyman shoemaker had less value as well. He had learned to perform each step of the shoemaker's craft, from

After the Revolutionary War shoemaking moved toward mass production, and many more women and children joined the trade.

start to finish. However, less-skilled workers could now be hired to do each of those tasks separately.

Master shoemakers began losing their place in the community. More and more people were buying ready-made shoes, which were much cheaper than custom-made shoes. Many master shoemakers were forced to close their shops and go to work in a wholesale shoe shop or factory. This was a hard move to make. The shoemaker had once been his own master. He was used to planning his own day and deciding how to organize his work. Now he had to work under a boss and follow someone else's directions.

Shoemaking Machines

One by one, machines began to take the place of handcrafting. Many of these new machines were invented by shoemakers. The rolling machine came into widespread use around 1845. It replaced the shoemaker's task of pounding sole leather with a hammer on a lapstone. The machine's heavy rollers made the leather compact and solid. A year later Elias Howe of Massachusetts invented the sewing machine. In 1851 shoemaker John Nichols developed a different needle and thread for the machine so it could sew shoe leather. This put an end to hand sewing at home.

A machine to sew the soles onto the uppers came out in 1858. Shoemaker Lyman R. Blake invented it, and Gordon McKay improved it. The type of shoe it made was known as the McKay. Other machines split hides, cut leather, drove in pegs, and trimmed edges. These inventions did many jobs that had once been done by hand.

One shoemaking task seemed impossible to do by machine. That was lasting, or pulling the leather around wooden lasts and tacking it in place. One hundred years had passed since the end of the Revolutionary War. But skilled workers still did this complex task by hand. Then, in 1883, Jan Matzeliger invented a lasting machine. This invention changed the shoemaking industry forever. Hand lasters could make fifty pairs of shoes a day. But the new lasting machine could produce as many as seven hundred pairs of shoes in a ten-hour workday! This eliminated even more skilled workers and further reduced the price of shoes.

A Lasting Contribution

Jan Ernst Matzeliger (1852–1889) was born in Paramaribo, now in the South American country of Suriname. His mother was a black woman and former slave, and his father was a Dutch engineer. When he was ten, Jan went to work in his father's machinery shop. He was fascinated by machines and how they work. As a young adult he went to sea on a merchant ship. Then he heard that the shoe industry in Massachusetts was growing fast. So he moved there and took a job at a shoe factory in Lynn. For years he spent his nights working on a new invention. He was determined to make a machine that could perform the shoe-lasting process. At last he succeeded. Matzeliger introduced his lasting machine in 1883. Sadly, he had become weak and exhausted from working so hard. He developed tuberculosis and died at age thirty-seven.

Jan E. Matzeliger
Shoe Lasting Machine   No. 274,207
Patented March 20, 1883
29
Black Heritage USA

The End of an Era

The new inventions spread quickly throughout the industry. Every shoe factory had to have a full array of machines. Then the price of factory-made shoes dropped dramatically. Shoe factories in the eastern United States shipped millions of shoes all over the country. Americans were settling new territory in the West, and they all needed reasonably priced shoes.

What about master shoemakers? By the late 1800s there were still a few who knew the craft. They made shoes at home for an occasional customer. After all, some people still preferred custom-made shoes handcrafted by a master. Most shoemakers, however, had ended up working in shoe factories or quit shoemaking altogether.

Many things had changed since colonial times. Master craftspeople once had vital roles in the community. They supplied their neighbors with furniture, clothes, shoes, dishes, guns, wheels, and tools. Now factories were mass-producing these goods.

Community life was much different, too. Young men and women left their farms to find work in factory towns. Immigrants from other countries poured in, too. The newcomers lived in boardinghouses until they could afford to rent a house or a private apartment. Work hours were long, and the pay was low. Often everyone in the family had to work to make ends meet. Children worked at the factories from morning until night, just as their parents did. School was a luxury many families could not afford. When a man with children died, his sons and daughters often provided the entire family income.

The familiar shoemaker's shop of colonial times grew dusty and rundown. It was no longer a social meeting place. No one stopped by to chat about the news of the day. Like the shoemaker himself, this way of life had become a thing of the past.

Still, the shoemaker's trade kept a strong presence in American life. By the mid-1800s shoemaking was the nation's second-largest occupation after agriculture. Shoemakers played an active role in the nation's new industrialized society. Along with textile workers, shoe workers were among the first groups to form **labor unions**. Through the unions, workers were able to obtain benefits for people in all industries. That included better wages and working conditions, limits on work hours, and laws against child labor.

The shoemakers' work environment had changed dramatically since colonial times. Nevertheless, shoemakers continued to be a positive force in community life.

Glossary

apothecaries   druggists who mix ingredients to make medicines

apprentices   young people who train under a master craftsperson to learn a trade

awl   a shoemaker's tool with a wooden handle and a sharp metal point for punching holes in leather for sewing or stitching

barter   payment by the exchange of goods or services instead of with money

colonial   relating to colonies

colonies   territories that are ruled by the country that settles them

colonists   people who settle a new land for their home country

cordwainers   the old English term for shoemakers

currier   a craftsperson who treats leather to make it more durable and soft

itinerant   traveling from place to place

journeyman   a craftsperson who has completed an apprenticeship and is getting paid for day work

labor unions   workers' organizations formed to secure better wages, benefits, and working conditions

last   a foot-shaped form around which shoes are constructed

merchants   businesspeople who sell goods

tanner   a craftsperson who treats animal hides with tannin to preserve them

waxed ends   shoemaker's thread, with a wild boar's bristle on each end for sewing

wholesale   the production of goods to sell to stores rather than directly to customers

Find Out More

BOOKS

Kalman, Bobbie. *A Visual Dictionary of a Colonial Community*. New York: Crabtree Publishing, 2008.

Roberts, Russell. *Life in Colonial America*. Hockessin, DE: Mitchell Lane Publishers, 2007.

Stefoff, Rebecca. *Cities and Towns* (Colonial Life). Armonk, NY: M. E. Sharpe, 2008.

Winters, Kay, and Larry Day (illustrator). *Colonial Voices: Hear Them Speak*. New York: Dutton Children's Books, 2008.

WEBSITES

Colonial Kids: A Celebration of Life in the 1700s

http://library.thinkquest.org/J002611F/

Find out what colonial children wore, what their communities were like, and how they worked and played.

Colonial Williamsburg Trades

www.history.org/Almanack/life/trades/tradehdr.cfm

This site explains many skilled trades in colonial times, including shoemaking.

Making Shoes and Boots

www.gpschools.org/ci/ce/elem/fifth/ss5/trades/cobbler.htm

Here you will find step-by-step photos of the shoemaking process in colonial days.

Index

Page numbers in **boldface** are illustrations.

About the Author

Ann Heinrichs is the author of more than two hundred books for children and young adults. Most of them cover U.S. and world history, geography, culture, and political affairs. Heinrichs was a children's book editor for many years. Then she worked as an advertising copywriter. An avid traveler, she has toured Europe, Asia, Africa, and the Middle East. Born in Fort Smith, Arkansas, she now lives in Chicago, Illinois. She enjoys bicycling and kayaking.